TABLE OF CONTENTS

45

46

47

48

49

50

51

52

53

54

55

56

57

58

59

60

61

62

63

64

65

66

67

68

69

70

71

72

73

74

75

76

77

78

79

80

81

82

83

84

85

86

87

88

89	95
90	96
91	97
92	98
93	99
94	100

Site / Account Name:

Example Account

Website: www.examplesite.com

User Name: johndoe

eMail: john@doe.com

Membership / Rewards #:
12345678910

Password: ~~0987654321~~ Date: ~~01/01/2010~~

Password: ~~newpassword~~ Date: ~~01/01/2015~~

Password: Strong@password2 Date: 01/01/2019

Password: Date:

Password: Date:

Password: Date:

Pin#: 1234

Secret Word: winning

Pass-phrase: welcome home

Phone# (associated with account): 949-123-4567

Address: 1234 Main St.
Somewhere, CA
92340

Notes:

Banking website for my retirement.

Site / Account Name:

Website:

User Name:

eMail:

Membership / Rewards #:

Password: Date:

Password: Date:

Password: Date:

Password: Date:

Password: Date:

Password: Date:

Pin#:

Secret Word:

Pass-phrase:

Phone# (associated with account):

Address:

Notes:

Site / Account Name:

Website:

User Name:

eMail:

Membership / Rewards #:

Password: Date:

Password: Date:

Password: Date:

Password: Date:

Password: Date:

Password: Date:

Pin#:

Secret Word:

Pass-phrase:

Phone# (associated with account):

Address:

Notes:

Site / Account Name:

Website:

User Name:

eMail:

Membership / Rewards #:

Password: Date:

Password: Date:

Password: Date:

Password: Date:

Password: Date:

Password: Date:

Pin#:

Secret Word:

Pass-phrase:

Phone# (associated with account):

Address:

Notes:

Site / Account Name:

Website:

User Name:

eMail:

Membership / Rewards #:

Password: Date:

Password: Date:

Password: Date:

Password: Date:

Password: Date:

Password: Date:

Pin#:

Secret Word:

Pass-phrase:

Phone# (associated with account):

Address:

Notes:

Site / Account Name:

Website:

User Name:

eMail:

Membership / Rewards #:

Password: Date:

Password: Date:

Password: Date:

Password: Date:

Password: Date:

Password: Date:

Pin#:

Secret Word:

Pass-phrase:

Phone# (associated with account):

Address:

Notes:

Site / Account Name:

Website:

User Name:

eMail:

Membership / Rewards #:

Password: Date:

Password: Date:

Password: Date:

Password: Date:

Password: Date:

Password: Date:

Pin#:

Secret Word:

Pass-phrase:

Phone# (associated with account):

Address:

Notes:

Site / Account Name:

Website:

User Name:

eMail:

Membership / Rewards #:

Password: Date:

Password: Date:

Password: Date:

Password: Date:

Password: Date:

Password: Date:

Pin#:

Secret Word:

Pass-phrase:

Phone# (associated with account):

Address:

Notes:

Site / Account Name:

Website:

User Name:

eMail:

Membership / Rewards #:

Password: Date:

Password: Date:

Password: Date:

Password: Date:

Password: Date:

Password: Date:

Pin#:

Secret Word:

Pass-phrase:

Phone# (associated with account):

Address:

Notes:

Site / Account Name:

Website:

User Name:

eMail:

Membership / Rewards #:

Password: Date:

Password: Date:

Password: Date:

Password: Date:

Password: Date:

Password: Date:

Pin#:

Secret Word:

Pass-phrase:

Phone# (associated with account):

Address:

Notes:

Site / Account Name:

Website:

User Name:

eMail:

Membership / Rewards #:

Password: Date:

Password: Date:

Password: Date:

Password: Date:

Password: Date:

Password: Date:

Pin#:

Secret Word:

Pass-phrase:

Phone# (associated with account):

Address:

Notes:

Site / Account Name:

Website:

User Name:

eMail:

Membership / Rewards #:

Password: Date:

Password: Date:

Password: Date:

Password: Date:

Password: Date:

Password: Date:

Pin#:

Secret Word:

Pass-phrase:

Phone# (associated with account):

Address:

Notes:

Site / Account Name:

Website:

User Name:

eMail:

Membership / Rewards #:

Password: Date:

Password: Date:

Password: Date:

Password: Date:

Password: Date:

Password: Date:

Pin#:

Secret Word:

Pass-phrase:

Phone# (associated with account):

Address:

Notes:

Site / Account Name:

Website:

User Name:

eMail:

Membership / Rewards #:

Password: Date:

Password: Date:

Password: Date:

Password: Date:

Password: Date:

Password: Date:

Pin#:

Secret Word:

Pass-phrase:

Phone# (associated with account):

Address:

Notes:

Site / Account Name:

Website:

User Name:

eMail:

Membership / Rewards #:

Password: Date:

Password: Date:

Password: Date:

Password: Date:

Password: Date:

Password: Date:

Pin#:

Secret Word:

Pass-phrase:

Phone# (associated with account):

Address:

Notes:

Site / Account Name:

Website:

User Name:

eMail:

Membership / Rewards #:

Password: Date:

Password: Date:

Password: Date:

Password: Date:

Password: Date:

Password: Date:

Pin#:

Secret Word:

Pass-phrase:

Phone# (associated with account):

Address:

Notes:

Site / Account Name:

Website:

User Name:

eMail:

Membership / Rewards #:

Password: Date:

Password: Date:

Password: Date:

Password: Date:

Password: Date:

Password: Date:

Pin#:

Secret Word:

Pass-phrase:

Phone# (associated with account):

Address:

Notes:

Site / Account Name:

Website:

User Name:

eMail:

Membership / Rewards #:

Password: Date:

Password: Date:

Password: Date:

Password: Date:

Password: Date:

Password: Date:

Pin#:

Secret Word:

Pass-phrase:

Phone# (associated with account):

Address:

Notes:

Site / Account Name:

Website:

User Name:

eMail:

Membership / Rewards #:

Password: Date:

Password: Date:

Password: Date:

Password: Date:

Password: Date:

Password: Date:

Pin#:

Secret Word:

Pass-phrase:

Phone# (associated with account):

Address:

Notes:

Site / Account Name:

Website:

User Name:

eMail:

Membership / Rewards #:

Password: Date:

Password: Date:

Password: Date:

Password: Date:

Password: Date:

Password: Date:

Pin#:

Secret Word:

Pass-phrase:

Phone# (associated with account):

Address:

Notes:

Site / Account Name:

Website:

User Name:

eMail:

Membership / Rewards #:

Password: Date:

Password: Date:

Password: Date:

Password: Date:

Password: Date:

Password: Date:

Pin#:

Secret Word:

Pass-phrase:

Phone# (associated with account):

Address:

Notes:

Site / Account Name:

Website:

User Name:

eMail:

Membership / Rewards #:

Password: Date:

Password: Date:

Password: Date:

Password: Date:

Password: Date:

Password: Date:

Pin#:

Secret Word:

Pass-phrase:

Phone# (associated with account):

Address:

Notes:

Site / Account Name:

Website:

User Name:

eMail:

Membership / Rewards #:

Password: Date:

Password: Date:

Password: Date:

Password: Date:

Password: Date:

Password: Date:

Pin#:

Secret Word:

Pass-phrase:

Phone# (associated with account):

Address:

Notes:

Site / Account Name:

Website:

User Name:

eMail:

Membership / Rewards #:

Password: Date:

Password: Date:

Password: Date:

Password: Date:

Password: Date:

Password: Date:

Pin#:

Secret Word:

Pass-phrase:

Phone# (associated with account):

Address:

Notes:

Site / Account Name:

Website:

User Name:

eMail:

Membership / Rewards #:

Password: Date:

Password: Date:

Password: Date:

Password: Date:

Password: Date:

Password: Date:

Pin#:

Secret Word:

Pass-phrase:

Phone# (associated with account):

Address:

Notes:

Site / Account Name:

Website:

User Name:

eMail:

Membership / Rewards #:

Password: Date:

Password: Date:

Password: Date:

Password: Date:

Password: Date:

Password: Date:

Pin#:

Secret Word:

Pass-phrase:

Phone# (associated with account):

Address:

Notes:

Site / Account Name:

Website:

User Name:

eMail:

Membership / Rewards #:

Password: Date:

Password: Date:

Password: Date:

Password: Date:

Password: Date:

Password: Date:

Pin#:

Secret Word:

Pass-phrase:

Phone# (associated with account):

Address:

Notes:

Site / Account Name:

Website:

User Name:

eMail:

Membership / Rewards #:

Password: Date:

Password: Date:

Password: Date:

Password: Date:

Password: Date:

Password: Date:

Pin#:

Secret Word:

Pass-phrase:

Phone# (associated with account):

Address:

Notes:

Site / Account Name:

Website:

User Name:

eMail:

Membership / Rewards #:

Password: Date:

Password: Date:

Password: Date:

Password: Date:

Password: Date:

Password: Date:

Pin#:

Secret Word:

Pass-phrase:

Phone# (associated with account):

Address:

Notes:

Site / Account Name:

Website:

User Name:

eMail:

Membership / Rewards #:

Password: Date:

Password: Date:

Password: Date:

Password: Date:

Password: Date:

Password: Date:

Pin#:

Secret Word:

Pass-phrase:

Phone# (associated with account):

Address:

Notes:

Site / Account Name:

Website:

User Name:

eMail:

Membership / Rewards #:

Password: Date:

Password: Date:

Password: Date:

Password: Date:

Password: Date:

Password: Date:

Pin#:

Secret Word:

Pass-phrase:

Phone# (associated with account):

Address:

Notes:

Site / Account Name:

Website:

User Name:

eMail:

Membership / Rewards #:

Password: Date:

Password: Date:

Password: Date:

Password: Date:

Password: Date:

Password: Date:

Pin#:

Secret Word:

Pass-phrase:

Phone# (associated with account):

Address:

Notes:

Site / Account Name:

Website:

User Name:

eMail:

Membership / Rewards #:

Password: Date:

Password: Date:

Password: Date:

Password: Date:

Password: Date:

Password: Date:

Pin#:

Secret Word:

Pass-phrase:

Phone# (associated with account):

Address:

Notes:

Site / Account Name:

Website:

User Name:

eMail:

Membership / Rewards #:

Password: Date:

Password: Date:

Password: Date:

Password: Date:

Password: Date:

Password: Date:

Pin#:

Secret Word:

Pass-phrase:

Phone# (associated with account):

Address:

Notes:

Site / Account Name:

Website:

User Name:

eMail:

Membership / Rewards #:

Password: Date:

Password: Date:

Password: Date:

Password: Date:

Password: Date:

Password: Date:

Pin#:

Secret Word:

Pass-phrase:

Phone# (associated with account):

Address:

Notes:

Site / Account Name:

Website:

User Name:

eMail:

Membership / Rewards #:

Password: Date:

Password: Date:

Password: Date:

Password: Date:

Password: Date:

Password: Date:

Pin#:

Secret Word:

Pass-phrase:

Phone# (associated with account):

Address:

Notes:

Site / Account Name:

Website:

User Name:

eMail:

Membership / Rewards #:

Password: Date:

Password: Date:

Password: Date:

Password: Date:

Password: Date:

Password: Date:

Pin#:

Secret Word:

Pass-phrase:

Phone# (associated with account):

Address:

Notes:

Site / Account Name:

Website:

User Name:

eMail:

Membership / Rewards #:

Password: Date:

Password: Date:

Password: Date:

Password: Date:

Password: Date:

Password: Date:

Pin#:

Secret Word:

Pass-phrase:

Phone# (associated with account):

Address:

Notes:

Site / Account Name:

Website:

User Name:

eMail:

Membership / Rewards #:

Password: Date:

Password: Date:

Password: Date:

Password: Date:

Password: Date:

Password: Date:

Pin#:

Secret Word:

Pass-phrase:

Phone# (associated with account):

Address:

Notes:

Site / Account Name:

Website:

User Name:

eMail:

Membership / Rewards #:

Password: Date:

Password: Date:

Password: Date:

Password: Date:

Password: Date:

Password: Date:

Pin#:

Secret Word:

Pass-phrase:

Phone# (associated with account):

Address:

Notes:

Site / Account Name:

Website:

User Name:

eMail:

Membership / Rewards #:

Password: Date:

Password: Date:

Password: Date:

Password: Date:

Password: Date:

Password: Date:

Pin#:

Notes:

Secret Word:

Pass-phrase:

Phone# (associated with account):

Address:

Site / Account Name:

Website:

User Name:

eMail:

Membership / Rewards #:

Password: Date:

Password: Date:

Password: Date:

Password: Date:

Password: Date:

Password: Date:

Pin#:

Secret Word:

Pass-phrase:

Phone# (associated with account):

Address:

Notes:

Site / Account Name:

Website:

User Name:

eMail:

Membership / Rewards #:

Password: Date:

Password: Date:

Password: Date:

Password: Date:

Password: Date:

Password: Date:

Pin#:

Secret Word:

Pass-phrase:

Phone# (associated with account):

Address:

Notes:

Site / Account Name:

Website:

User Name:

eMail:

Membership / Rewards #:

Password: Date:

Password: Date:

Password: Date:

Password: Date:

Password: Date:

Password: Date:

Pin#:

Notes:

Secret Word:

Pass-phrase:

Phone# (associated with account):

Address:

Site / Account Name:

Website:

User Name:

eMail:

Membership / Rewards #:

Password: Date:

Password: Date:

Password: Date:

Password: Date:

Password: Date:

Password: Date:

Pin#:

Secret Word:

Pass-phrase:

Phone# (associated with account):

Address:

Notes:

Site / Account Name:

Website:

User Name:

eMail:

Membership / Rewards #:

Password: Date:

Password: Date:

Password: Date:

Password: Date:

Password: Date:

Password: Date:

Pin#:

Secret Word:

Pass-phrase:

Phone# (associated with account):

Address:

Notes:

Site / Account Name:

Website:

User Name:

eMail:

Membership / Rewards #:

Password: Date:

Password: Date:

Password: Date:

Password: Date:

Password: Date:

Password: Date:

Pin#:

Secret Word:

Pass-phrase:

Phone# (associated with account):

Address:

Notes:

Site / Account Name:

Website:

User Name:

eMail:

Membership / Rewards #:

Password: Date:

Password: Date:

Password: Date:

Password: Date:

Password: Date:

Password: Date:

Pin#:

Secret Word:

Pass-phrase:

Phone# (associated with account):

Address:

Notes:

Site / Account Name:

Website:

User Name:

eMail:

Membership / Rewards #:

Password: Date:

Password: Date:

Password: Date:

Password: Date:

Password: Date:

Password: Date:

Pin#:

Secret Word:

Pass-phrase:

Phone# (associated with account):

Address:

Notes:

Site / Account Name:

Website:

User Name:

eMail:

Membership / Rewards #:

Password: Date:

Password: Date:

Password: Date:

Password: Date:

Password: Date:

Password: Date:

Pin#:

Secret Word:

Pass-phrase:

Phone# (associated with account):

Address:

Notes:

Site / Account Name:

Website:

User Name:

eMail:

Membership / Rewards #:

Password: Date:

Password: Date:

Password: Date:

Password: Date:

Password: Date:

Password: Date:

Pin#:

Secret Word:

Pass-phrase:

Phone# (associated with account):

Address:

Notes:

Site / Account Name:

Website:

User Name:

eMail:

Membership / Rewards #:

Password: Date:

Password: Date:

Password: Date:

Password: Date:

Password: Date:

Password: Date:

Pin#:

Secret Word:

Pass-phrase:

Phone# (associated with account):

Address:

Notes:

Site / Account Name:

Website:

User Name:

eMail:

Membership / Rewards #:

Password: Date:

Password: Date:

Password: Date:

Password: Date:

Password: Date:

Password: Date:

Pin#:

Secret Word:

Pass-phrase:

Phone# (associated with account):

Address:

Notes:

Site / Account Name:

Website:

User Name:

eMail:

Membership / Rewards #:

Password: Date:

Password: Date:

Password: Date:

Password: Date:

Password: Date:

Password: Date:

Pin#:

Secret Word:

Pass-phrase:

Phone# (associated with account):

Address:

Notes:

Site / Account Name:

Website:

User Name:

eMail:

Membership / Rewards #:

Password: Date:

Password: Date:

Password: Date:

Password: Date:

Password: Date:

Password: Date:

Pin#:

Secret Word:

Pass-phrase:

Phone# (associated with account):

Address:

Notes:

Site / Account Name:

Website:

User Name:

eMail:

Membership / Rewards #:

Password: Date:

Password: Date:

Password: Date:

Password: Date:

Password: Date:

Password: Date:

Pin#:

Secret Word:

Pass-phrase:

Phone# (associated with account):

Address:

Notes:

Site / Account Name:

Website:

User Name:

eMail:

Membership / Rewards #:

Password: Date:

Password: Date:

Password: Date:

Password: Date:

Password: Date:

Password: Date:

Pin#:

Secret Word:

Pass-phrase:

Phone# (associated with account):

Address:

Notes:

Site / Account Name:

Website:

User Name:

eMail:

Membership / Rewards #:

Password: Date:

Password: Date:

Password: Date:

Password: Date:

Password: Date:

Password: Date:

Pin#:

Secret Word:

Pass-phrase:

Phone# (associated with account):

Address:

Notes:

Site / Account Name:

Website:

User Name:

eMail:

Membership / Rewards #:

Password: Date:

Password: Date:

Password: Date:

Password: Date:

Password: Date:

Password: Date:

Pin#:

Secret Word:

Pass-phrase:

Phone# (associated with account):

Address:

Notes:

Site / Account Name:

Website:

User Name:

eMail:

Membership / Rewards #:

Password: Date:

Password: Date:

Password: Date:

Password: Date:

Password: Date:

Password: Date:

Pin#:

Secret Word:

Pass-phrase:

Phone# (associated with account):

Address:

Notes:

Site / Account Name:

Website:

User Name:

eMail:

Membership / Rewards #:

Password: Date:

Password: Date:

Password: Date:

Password: Date:

Password: Date:

Password: Date:

Pin#:

Secret Word:

Pass-phrase:

Phone# (associated with account):

Address:

Notes:

Site / Account Name:

Website:

User Name:

eMail:

Membership / Rewards #:

Password: Date:

Password: Date:

Password: Date:

Password: Date:

Password: Date:

Password: Date:

Pin#:

Secret Word:

Pass-phrase:

Phone# (associated with account):

Address:

Notes:

Site / Account Name:

Website:

User Name:

eMail:

Membership / Rewards #:

Password: Date:

Password: Date:

Password: Date:

Password: Date:

Password: Date:

Password: Date:

Pin#:

Secret Word:

Pass-phrase:

Phone# (associated with account):

Address:

Notes:

Site / Account Name:

Website:

User Name:

eMail:

Membership / Rewards #:

Password: Date:

Password: Date:

Password: Date:

Password: Date:

Password: Date:

Password: Date:

Pin#:

Secret Word:

Pass-phrase:

Phone# (associated with account):

Address:

Notes:

Site / Account Name:

Website:

User Name:

eMail:

Membership / Rewards #:

Password: Date:

Password: Date:

Password: Date:

Password: Date:

Password: Date:

Password: Date:

Pin#:

Secret Word:

Pass-phrase:

Phone# (associated with account):

Address:

Notes:

Site / Account Name:

Website:

User Name:

eMail:

Membership / Rewards #:

Password: Date:

Password: Date:

Password: Date:

Password: Date:

Password: Date:

Password: Date:

Pin#:

Secret Word:

Pass-phrase:

Phone# (associated with account):

Address:

Notes:

Site / Account Name:

Website:

User Name:

eMail:

Membership / Rewards #:

Password: Date:

Password: Date:

Password: Date:

Password: Date:

Password: Date:

Password: Date:

Pin#:

Secret Word:

Pass-phrase:

Phone# (associated with account):

Address:

Notes:

Site / Account Name:

Website:

User Name:

eMail:

Membership / Rewards #:

Password: Date:

Password: Date:

Password: Date:

Password: Date:

Password: Date:

Password: Date:

Pin#:

Secret Word:

Pass-phrase:

Phone# (associated with account):

Address:

Notes:

Site / Account Name:

Website:

User Name:

eMail:

Membership / Rewards #:

Password: Date:

Password: Date:

Password: Date:

Password: Date:

Password: Date:

Password: Date:

Pin#:

Secret Word:

Pass-phrase:

Phone# (associated with account):

Address:

Notes:

Site / Account Name:

Website:

User Name:

eMail:

Membership / Rewards #:

Password: Date:

Password: Date:

Password: Date:

Password: Date:

Password: Date:

Password: Date:

Pin#:

Secret Word:

Pass-phrase:

Phone# (associated with account):

Address:

Notes:

Site / Account Name:

Website:

User Name:

eMail:

Membership / Rewards #:

Password: Date:

Password: Date:

Password: Date:

Password: Date:

Password: Date:

Password: Date:

Pin#:

Secret Word:

Pass-phrase:

Phone# (associated with account):

Address:

Notes:

Site / Account Name:

Website:

User Name:

eMail:

Membership / Rewards #:

Password: Date:

Password: Date:

Password: Date:

Password: Date:

Password: Date:

Password: Date:

Pin#:

Secret Word:

Pass-phrase:

Phone# (associated with account):

Address:

Notes:

Site / Account Name:

Website:

User Name:

eMail:

Membership / Rewards #:

Password: Date:

Password: Date:

Password: Date:

Password: Date:

Password: Date:

Password: Date:

Pin#:

Secret Word:

Pass-phrase:

Phone# (associated with account):

Address:

Notes:

Site / Account Name:

Website:

User Name:

eMail:

Membership / Rewards #:

Password: Date:

Password: Date:

Password: Date:

Password: Date:

Password: Date:

Password: Date:

Pin#:

Secret Word:

Pass-phrase:

Phone# (associated with account):

Address:

Notes:

Site / Account Name:

Website:

User Name:

eMail:

Membership / Rewards #:

Password: Date:

Password: Date:

Password: Date:

Password: Date:

Password: Date:

Password: Date:

Pin#:

Secret Word:

Pass-phrase:

Phone# (associated with account):

Address:

Notes:

Site / Account Name:

Website:

User Name:

eMail:

Membership / Rewards #:

Password: Date:

Password: Date:

Password: Date:

Password: Date:

Password: Date:

Password: Date:

Pin#:

Secret Word:

Pass-phrase:

Phone# (associated with account):

Address:

Notes:

Site / Account Name:

Website:

User Name:

eMail:

Membership / Rewards #:

Password: Date:

Password: Date:

Password: Date:

Password: Date:

Password: Date:

Password: Date:

Pin#:

Secret Word:

Pass-phrase:

Phone# (associated with account):

Address:

Notes:

Site / Account Name:

Website:

User Name:

eMail:

Membership / Rewards #:

Password: Date:

Password: Date:

Password: Date:

Password: Date:

Password: Date:

Password: Date:

Pin#:

Secret Word:

Pass-phrase:

Phone# (associated with account):

Address:

Notes:

Site / Account Name:

Website:

User Name:

eMail:

Membership / Rewards #:

Password: Date:

Password: Date:

Password: Date:

Password: Date:

Password: Date:

Password: Date:

Pin#:

Secret Word:

Pass-phrase:

Phone# (associated with account):

Address:

Notes:

Site / Account Name:

Website:

User Name:

eMail:

Membership / Rewards #:

Password: Date:

Password: Date:

Password: Date:

Password: Date:

Password: Date:

Password: Date:

Pin#:

Secret Word:

Pass-phrase:

Phone# (associated with account):

Address:

Notes:

Site / Account Name:

Website:

User Name:

eMail:

Membership / Rewards #:

Password: Date:

Password: Date:

Password: Date:

Password: Date:

Password: Date:

Password: Date:

Pin#:

Secret Word:

Pass-phrase:

Phone# (associated with account):

Address:

Notes:

Site / Account Name:

Website:

User Name:

eMail:

Membership / Rewards #:

Password: Date:

Password: Date:

Password: Date:

Password: Date:

Password: Date:

Password: Date:

Pin#:

Secret Word:

Pass-phrase:

Phone# (associated with account):

Address:

Notes:

Site / Account Name:

Website:

User Name:

eMail:

Membership / Rewards #:

Password: Date:

Password: Date:

Password: Date:

Password: Date:

Password: Date:

Password: Date:

Pin#:

Secret Word:

Pass-phrase:

Phone# (associated with account):

Address:

Notes:

Site / Account Name:

Website:

User Name:

eMail:

Membership / Rewards #:

Password: Date:

Password: Date:

Password: Date:

Password: Date:

Password: Date:

Password: Date:

Pin#:

Secret Word:

Pass-phrase:

Phone# (associated with account):

Address:

Notes:

Site / Account Name:

Website:

User Name:

eMail:

Membership / Rewards #:

Password: Date:

Password: Date:

Password: Date:

Password: Date:

Password: Date:

Password: Date:

Pin#:

Secret Word:

Pass-phrase:

Phone# (associated with account):

Address:

Notes:

Site / Account Name:

Website:

User Name:

eMail:

Membership / Rewards #:

Password: Date:

Password: Date:

Password: Date:

Password: Date:

Password: Date:

Password: Date:

Pin#:

Secret Word:

Pass-phrase:

Phone# (associated with account):

Address:

Notes:

Site / Account Name:

Website:

User Name:

eMail:

Membership / Rewards #:

Password: Date:

Password: Date:

Password: Date:

Password: Date:

Password: Date:

Password: Date:

Pin#:

Secret Word:

Pass-phrase:

Phone# (associated with account):

Address:

Notes:

Site / Account Name:

Website:

User Name:

eMail:

Membership / Rewards #:

Password: Date:

Password: Date:

Password: Date:

Password: Date:

Password: Date:

Password: Date:

Pin#:

Secret Word:

Pass-phrase:

Phone# (associated with account):

Address:

Notes:

Site / Account Name:

Website:

User Name:

eMail:

Membership / Rewards #:

Password: Date:

Password: Date:

Password: Date:

Password: Date:

Password: Date:

Password: Date:

Pin#:

Secret Word:

Pass-phrase:

Phone# (associated with account):

Address:

Notes:

Site / Account Name:

Website:

User Name:

eMail:

Membership / Rewards #:

Password: Date:

Password: Date:

Password: Date:

Password: Date:

Password: Date:

Password: Date:

Pin#:

Secret Word:

Pass-phrase:

Phone# (associated with account):

Address:

Notes:

Site / Account Name:

Website:

User Name:

eMail:

Membership / Rewards #:

Password: Date:

Password: Date:

Password: Date:

Password: Date:

Password: Date:

Password: Date:

Pin#:

Secret Word:

Pass-phrase:

Phone# (associated with account):

Address:

Notes:

Site / Account Name:

Website:

User Name:

eMail:

Membership / Rewards #:

Password: Date:

Password: Date:

Password: Date:

Password: Date:

Password: Date:

Password: Date:

Pin#:

Secret Word:

Pass-phrase:

Phone# (associated with account):

Address:

Notes:

Site / Account Name:

Website:

User Name:

eMail:

Membership / Rewards #:

Password: Date:

Password: Date:

Password: Date:

Password: Date:

Password: Date:

Password: Date:

Pin#:

Secret Word:

Pass-phrase:

Phone# (associated with account):

Address:

Notes:

Site / Account Name:

Website:

User Name:

eMail:

Membership / Rewards #:

Password: Date:

Password: Date:

Password: Date:

Password: Date:

Password: Date:

Password: Date:

Pin#:

Secret Word:

Pass-phrase:

Phone# (associated with account):

Address:

Notes:

Site / Account Name:

Website:

User Name:

eMail:

Membership / Rewards #:

Password: Date:

Password: Date:

Password: Date:

Password: Date:

Password: Date:

Password: Date:

Pin#:

Secret Word:

Pass-phrase:

Phone# (associated with account):

Address:

Notes:

Site / Account Name:

Website:

User Name:

eMail:

Membership / Rewards #:

Password: Date:

Password: Date:

Password: Date:

Password: Date:

Password: Date:

Password: Date:

Pin#:

Secret Word:

Pass-phrase:

Phone# (associated with account):

Address:

Notes:

Site / Account Name:

Website:

User Name:

eMail:

Membership / Rewards #:

Password: Date:

Password: Date:

Password: Date:

Password: Date:

Password: Date:

Password: Date:

Pin#:

Secret Word:

Pass-phrase:

Phone# (associated with account):

Address:

Notes:

Site / Account Name:

Website:

User Name:

eMail:

Membership / Rewards #:

Password: Date:

Password: Date:

Password: Date:

Password: Date:

Password: Date:

Password: Date:

Pin#:

Secret Word:

Pass-phrase:

Phone# (associated with account):

Address:

Notes:

Site / Account Name:

Website:

User Name:

eMail:

Membership / Rewards #:

Password: Date:

Password: Date:

Password: Date:

Password: Date:

Password: Date:

Password: Date:

Pin#:

Secret Word:

Pass-phrase:

Phone# (associated with account):

Address:

Notes:

Site / Account Name:

Website:

User Name:

eMail:

Membership / Rewards #:

Password: Date:

Password: Date:

Password: Date:

Password: Date:

Password: Date:

Password: Date:

Pin#:

Secret Word:

Pass-phrase:

Phone# (associated with account):

Address:

Notes:

Site / Account Name:

Website:

User Name:

eMail:

Membership / Rewards #:

Password: Date:

Password: Date:

Password: Date:

Password: Date:

Password: Date:

Password: Date:

Pin#:

Secret Word:

Pass-phrase:

Phone# (associated with account):

Address:

Notes:

Made in the USA
Monee, IL
04 November 2026

67384416R00059